*Dedicated to the memory
of Marion L. Quimby
who through her God-given
artistic talent was
instrumental in pioneering
our inspirational series
of books.
Her legacy will live on
through her beautiful
works of art.*

*Art is beauty made a sacrament.
Art is finite human expression made
infinite by love.*

                            V. McNabb

Salesian Missions wishes to thank those who have given their kind permission to reprint material included in this book. Every effort has been made to give proper acknowledgements. Any omissions or errors are deeply regretted, and the publisher, upon notification, will be pleased to make necessary corrections in subsequent editions.

Poems of Hope

from the Salesian Collection

Compiled and Edited by
Sara Tarascio

·

Illustrated by
Marion L. Quimby
Paul Scully
Frank Massa
and
Russell D. Bushée

CONTENTS

God Is Never Beyond Our Reach

No one ever sought the Father
And found He was not there,
And no burden is too heavy
To be lightened by a prayer,
No problem is too intricate
And no sorrow that we face
Is too deep and devastating
To be softened by His grace,
No trials and tribulations
Are beyond what we can bear
If we share them with our Father
As we talk to Him in prayer —
And men of every color,
Every race and every creed
Have but to seek the Father
In their deepest hour of need —

God asks for no credentials,
He accepts us with our flaws,
He is kind and understanding
And He welcomes us because
We are His erring children
And He loves us everyone,
And He freely and completely
Forgives all that we have done,
Asking only if we're ready
To follow where He leads —
Content that in His wisdom
He will answer all our needs.

Helen Steiner Rice

Used with permission of
The Helen Steiner Rice Foundation
Suite 2100 Atrium Two
221 E. Fourth St.
Cincinnati, OH 45202

In Harmony With Nature

There are wonders all around us
To see, to touch, to hear —
God's handiwork surrounds us
And reminds us He is near . . .
So every time you smell a flower,
Or see a starlit sky,
Or hear a cricket chirping,
Or feel a breeze blow by,
Or witness all the splendor
A changing season brings,
You've touched the hand of God above —
The Creator of all things!

Alice Joyce Davidson

Pack Away Your Troubles

Face your day with a happy heart
   And end it with a song—
You'll find the hours in between
   Can't go far from wrong.

A smile is more contagious
   Than a dreary frown,
And nicer to remember
   When the sun goes down.

Don't miss out on happiness
   By looking toward the ground—
But keep looking skyward,
   That's where the rainbow's found.

Just pack away your troubles
   For some other day
And before you know it,
   They'll have slipped away.

Catherine Janssen Irwin

Born for Joy

God gives us the sunset in the sky
And colors the wings of each butterfly.
Does He not love us?

His stars are bright in the darkest night
And His holy angels guide us aright.
Does He not love us?

He offered His son that we may be
With Him in His glory eternally.
Does He not love us?

Our true home is fairer than this earth
And it is for heaven God gave us birth.
Does He not love us?

Sr. Mary Gemma Brunke

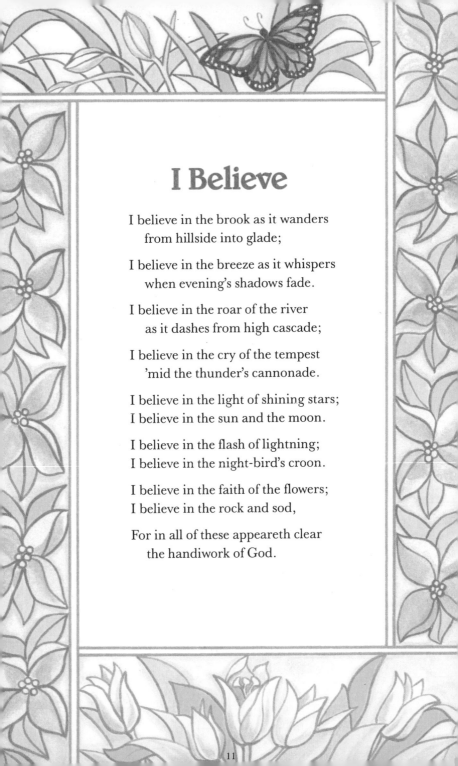

I Believe

I believe in the brook as it wanders
   from hillside into glade;

I believe in the breeze as it whispers
   when evening's shadows fade.

I believe in the roar of the river
   as it dashes from high cascade;

I believe in the cry of the tempest
   'mid the thunder's cannonade.

I believe in the light of shining stars;
I believe in the sun and the moon.

I believe in the flash of lightning;
I believe in the night-bird's croon.

I believe in the faith of the flowers;
I believe in the rock and sod,

For in all of these appeareth clear
   the handiwork of God.

His Sunshine

There's sunshine in my heart today
because He walks with me.
He fills my life with rainbow hues;
He sets my spirit free.

When shadows seek to cross my path
blocking His sun rays,
I turn my thoughts to blessings given
and lift my heart in praise.

Even in the darkest times,
His blessings still remain —
No matter what may come my way,
Praise God! His love's the same.

He's promised always to be there;
what comfort to my soul.
How precious is His tender care
no greater joy I hold.

He's the light that fills my world
though skies are not so blue
and even on the darkest days
His sunshine still peeks through.

                    Jeri Sweany

Don't Quit

When things go wrong as they sometimes will,
When the road you're trudging seems all up hill,
When the funds are low and the debts are high,
And you want to smile, but you have to sigh,
When care is pressing you down a bit,
Rest if you must, but don't you quit.

Life is queer with its twists and turns,
As everyone of us sometimes learns,
And many a failure turns about
When he might have won had he stuck it out;
Don't give up though the pace seems slow
You may succeed with another blow.

Success is failure turned inside out —
The silver tint of the clouds of doubt,
And you never can tell just how close you are,
It may be near when it seems so far;
So stick to the fight when you're hardest hit —
It's when things seem worst
that you must not quit.

Make Your Day Bright

Don't start your day by supposin'
   that trouble is just ahead,
It's better to stop supposin'
   and start with a prayer instead,
And make it a prayer of thanksgiving
   for the wonderful things God has wrought
Like the beautiful sunrise and sunset,
   "God's Gifts" that are free
   and not bought —
For what is the use of supposin'
   the dire things that could happen to you
And worry about some misfortune
   that seldom if ever comes true —
But instead of just idle supposin'
   step forward to meet each new day
Secure in the knowledge God's near you
   to lead you each step of the way —
For supposin' the worst things will happen
   only helps to make them come true
And you darken the bright, happy moments
   that the dear Lord has given to you —
So if you desire to be happy
   and get rid of the "misery of dread"
Just give up "supposin' the worst things"
   and look for "the best things" instead.

Helen Steiner Rice

Used with permission of
The Helen Steiner Rice Foundation
Suite 2100 Atrium Two
221 E. Fourth St.
Cincinnati, OH 45202

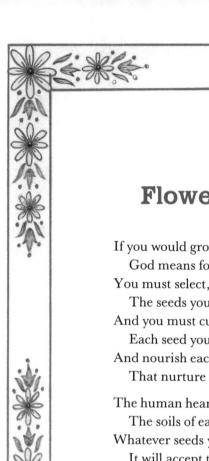

Flowers of Love

If you would grow the "Flowers Of Love" —
   God means for you to grow —
You must select, with special care,
   The seeds you plant and sow;
And you must cultivate with love,
   Each seed you want to flower,
And nourish each with gentle ways
   That nurture and endower.

The human heart is not unlike
   The soils of earth we sow.
Whatever seeds you choose to plant,
   It will accept to grow —
So you must plant with careful choice
   (What you would have them bear)
And plant the loves you want to reap —
   When flowers blossom there.

               Michael Dubina

Give Me

God, give me eyes that I might see
   The work that can be done by me;
God, give me ears that I might hear
   The cry of those who need me near.
God, give me lips that I might speak
   Comfort and peace to all who seek;
God, give me a mind that I might know
   How to help those who need me so.

God, give me hands that I might do
   Some large or simple task for You;
God, give me a prayer that I might pray
   Thy help and guidance every day.
And this one thing, all else above;
God, give me a heart that I may love.

The Lord be with you as you walk
   Along your homeward road.
In silent thought, in friendly talk,
   May you be near to God.
The Lord be with you as the night
   Enfolds your day with rest.
Be He in every heart the light,
   In every home the guest.

Love at Home

There is beauty all around
When there's love at home;
There is joy in every sound
When there's love at home.

Peace and plenty here abide,
Smiling sweet on every side;
Time doth softly, sweetly glide
When there's love at home.

Teach Me

Teach me, O Lord, to be sweet and gentle
    In all the events of life; in
Disappointments, in the thoughtlessness
    Of others, in the insincerity of those
I trusted, in the unfaithfulness of those
    On whom I relied. Teach me to profit by
The suffering that comes across my path.
    May no one be less good for having
Come within my influence; no one less
    Pure, less true, less kind, less noble for
Having been a fellow-traveler in our
    Journey toward Eternal life.

Gentle Love

A whisp of wind,
A glimmer of gold,
The Hand of God,
Of love unfolds,

Raindrops of hope,
Dewdrops of care,
Gentle reminders,
God's Hand everywhere.

Mary Pederson

Positive Living

A new start, a bright new beginning
To start all over again,
In friendship and positive living,
Greeting each day with a song.
So many moments to treasure,
So many joys to give,
A kindness, or bit of pleasure
To scatter and to receive.
Why live one day in regretting
The deeds that were left undone,
Instead, just go right on loving,
And happiness surely will come.

Elsie Natalie Brady

Atonement

Help me, Lord, to make amends
    To those I may have hurt.
So often without thinking
    Remarks I make are curt.
Teach me to be sensitive
    To other persons' needs,
That I may speak with kindness
    And follow with this creed.

Helen Parker

The
Purged Branch

Each branch
of the Vine that is Christ
bears the purging,
to bring forth
fruit of the Spirit
for abundant
and eternal life.

Edward A. Gloeggler

The Challenge

Do you think that your tomorrow
   Will be different than today?
Do you think the things you hoped for
   Will come true in any way?

By the thoughts you put in action,
By the dreams you strive to reach —
   You can shape or form the future
   By some hard-sought fact they teach.

Choose the good you want to happen —
   It surrounds you in the "now".
You can make or change the present . . .
Let God's wisdom show you how!

   Take the path that seems to open:
For you're walking it today!
You can even change tomorrow
If you let God show the way!

Roxie Lusk Smith

We Have to Ask

We have to ask God's help,
For though He sees
Into the dark recesses of each mind,
He wants to hear the words,
Our lips were made
For supplications of this very kind.
We have to ask God's help,
To let Him know
We are too weak to walk the way alone,
To go to Him in prayer when things become
Too much for us to handle on our own.

His eyes can penetrate the thickest fog,
His fingers can throw back the strongest lock,
How can we hope to ever enter in,
Unless we stand before the gate and knock?
For it is in the seeking that we find,
And through His aid alone, the meanest task,
Assumes its share of true nobility,
But grace is only given . . . if we ask.

Grace E. Easley

The Living Light

Today I noticed a brilliant light
   Shining across my way,
And I saw it was a beautiful
   Sun's bright golden ray.
It flickered there ever before me
   As though trying to show
Just the right way leading to where
   I was wishing to go.
And it made me think how we can be
   Free from worry and strife
If we follow the light of Jesus
   That falls 'cross the pathway of life.
     Virginia Katherine Oliver

Morning and Night

I say a prayer each morning and
I say one every night
Because somehow they make me feel
That everything is right.

They seem to give the golden sun
A warm and friendly glow
And draw a brighter moonbeam to
The flowers and the snow.

They sort of shape the silver stars
That twinkle in the sky
And give a breath of incense to
The winds that wander by.

My morning and my evening prayers
Are candle-wicks that burn
So I may walk the proper path
And know which way to turn.

And, after all I love my God
And it is only right
That I should take the time to say
Good morning and good night.

James J. Metcalfe

Little Things

It's all the little things that count,
To make a life, complete;
Common things; Simple things —
Life's struggles to defeat:

A word of hope;
A note of cheer;
A kiss to tender sorrow;
A thoughtful deed;
A smile of warmth;
A hand of help to borrow;
A faith in God;
A love for man;
A trust for joy and sorrow —

It's all these little things that count —
Today, and through tomorrow.

Michael Dubina

How Sweet the Sound

How sweet the sound of morning birds
that sing from summer trees
the melodies of nature
that comfort and appease.
How sweet the evening wind song
beside the restless sea
where the ages are but movements
in nature's symphony.
How sweet a mother's lullaby
by waning candlelight
as she holds within her arms
her miracle tonight.
How sweet the sounds of nature
throughout this earthly sod
where we have heard unknowing
the gentle voice of God.

Clay Harrison

Finding God

I looked for God this morning as
Dew glistened on the grass,
I stood beside the crossroads where
I thought He'd surely pass.
I strolled among the shadows of
A forest green with pine,
Through fragrant country gardens where
The morning glories twine.

I looked for God this afternoon,
Upon a sunny hill,
'Neath the skies of blue and down beside
A rustic watermill.
Upon the banks of narrow streams,
That wind their merry way
Past fertile fields of clover where
The happy children play.

I looked for God this evening,
As I was homeward bound,
Along a yellow gravel road
That took me back to town.
The wasted hours weighed upon
My shoulders heavily,
My footsteps dragged because God had
Not shown Himself to me.

And then a cool breeze fanned my face,
And through my tears the bright
Fluorescent glow of tiny stars,
That blazed across the night.
And in my soul a blessed peace,
For suddenly I knew,
One cannot walk with beauty, Lord,
And not discover You.

                    Grace E. Easley

Three Lessons

There are three lessons I would write—
   Three words as with a burning pen,
In tracings of eternal light,
   Upon the hearts of men.

Have Hope. Though clouds environ now,
   And gladness hides her face in scorn,
Put thou the shadow from thy brow—
   No night but hath its morn.

Have Faith. Where'er thy bark is driven—
   The calm's disport, the tempest's mirth—
Know this: God rules the host of heaven,
   The inhabitants of earth.

Have Love. Not love alone for one,
   But man as man thy brother call;
And scatter like the circling sun
   Thy charities on all.

Thus grave these lessons on thy soul—
   Faith, Hope, and Love—and thou shalt
     find
Strength when life's surges rudest roll,
   Light when thou else wert blind.

Johann Christopher Friedrich von Schiller

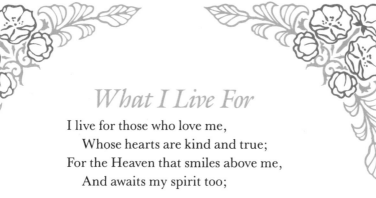

What I Live For

I live for those who love me,
   Whose hearts are kind and true;
For the Heaven that smiles above me,
   And awaits my spirit too;

For all human ties that bind me,
For the task by God assigned me,
For the bright hopes yet to find me,
   And the good that I can do.

I live to hold communion
   With all that is divine,
To feel there is a union
   'Twixt Nature's heart and mine;
To profit by affliction,
Reap truth from fields of fiction,
Grow wiser from conviction,
   And fulfill God's grand design.

I live for those who love me,
   For those who know me true;
For the heaven that smiles above me,
   And awaits my spirit too;
For the cause that lacks assistance,
For the wrong that needs resistance,
For the future in the distance,
   And the good that I can do.

           G. Linnaeus Banks

Helping Others

You gave on the way a pleasant smile
    And thought no more about it.
It cheered a life that had been dark the while
    Which might have been wrecked without it.
And so for that smile that was given there,
    You'll have a reward sometime — somewhere.

You spoke one day a cheering word,
    And passed to other duties.
It cheered a heart; new promise stirred
    And painted a life with beauties.
And so for that word of golden cheer,
    You'll have a reward sometime — somewhere.

You lent a hand to a fallen one;
    A lift in love was given.
You saved a soul when hope was gone
    And helped him on toward heaven.
And so, for that help you proffered there,
    You'll have a reward sometime — somewhere.

Friends Are for Caring

You can bring the sunshine
　To that dark and dreary day,
That engulfs a neighbor
　When sorrow comes his way.

Share the load he carries
　As you sip a cup of tea,
Give strong words of courage,
　Be the friend you'd like to be.

These few unselfish moments
　When you show you really care,
Will lead to treasured memories
　Of those times when you were there.

Catherine Janssen Irwin

When life seems just a
   dreary grind,
And things seem fated to
   annoy,
Say something nice to
   someone else —
And watch the world light
   up with joy!

The Vine

He is the vine, He is the life,
There is a boundless flow.
Oh infinite love that calls to me,
His wondrous grace to know.

He is the vine, I can depend
on Him to hold me fast.
I try so hard myself to stay,
My strength shall never last.

He is the vine, Himself He gives—
His riches too, full and free.
To His bosom with open arms
Is His welcome to me.

He is the vine, Oh blessed thought,
Grafted to His wounded side.
His strong love ever holds me fast
In Him I do abide.

Ken Peters

You're Never Alone

You're never alone, with Jesus,
   He's always by your side,

Giving strength, and wisdom,
   With you, He does abide,

To keep you safe from danger,
   The trials that come your way,

You're never alone, with Jesus,
   He's with you every day.

Colette Fedor

Influence

Drop a pebble in the water,
And its ripples reach out far;
And the sunbeams dancing on them
May reflect them to a star.

Give a smile to someone passing,
Thereby making his morning glad;
It may greet you in the evening
When your own heart may be sad.

Do a deed of simple kindness;
Though its end you may not see,
It may reach, like widening ripples,
Down a long eternity.

Joseph Norris

Dear God

The little plans I tried
to carry through
Have failed.
I will not sorrow.
I'll pause a little while,
Dear God,
    And try, again, tomorrow

Minutes of Gold

Two or three minutes—two or three hours,
What do they mean in this life of ours?
Not very much if but counted as time,
But minutes of gold and hours sublime,
If only we'll use them once in a while
To make someone happy—make someone smile.
A minute may dry a little lad's tears,
An hour sweep aside trouble of years.
Minutes of my time may bring to an end
Hopelessness somewhere, and bring me a friend.

Simple Soul

Lord let me be a simple soul,
No matter what life brings
Finding joy in solitude,
And peace in little things.
Content to watch the grasses grow,
And all the flowers bloom,
Bringing sunlight to the lives
That may be touched with gloom.

Lord let me be a simple soul,
However grand this earth,
And never let me once forget
How much my soul is worth.
Blind me to the things of life,
That cause the heart to stray,
And keep me just a simple soul,
. . . Forever and a day.

Grace E. Easley

A Time to Believe

A time to remember,
A time to forget,
A time to be happy,
A time for regret.
A time when all comforting
words cannot heal
the pain and the sorrow
that broken hearts feel.

But faith gives us courage,
And pray'r soothes it all,
The Savior will answer
Our feeblest call.
We've only to ask,
And His Blessings receive,
Hope for tomorrow,
A Time to Believe!

Bill Carr

If you want to be happy,
  Begin where you are,
Don't wait for some rapture
  That's future and far.
Begin to be joyous, begin to be glad
  And soon you'll forget
That you ever were sad.

When Evening Comes

Evening is a time to think
   and cast your cares aside;
A time to pray and meditate,
   and in the Lord, confide.

Evening is a time to read,
   write letters to a friend;
A time to sit with family,
   to visit, sew, or mend.

A time to ponder in your mind,
   and think your own thoughts
      through;
A time to cuddle little ones,
   and them, to cuddle you.

Evening is a time to dream,
   and sleep in Holy care,
And trust that God,
   is working nights
   to answer every prayer.

Roxie Lusk Smith

Little Sparrow

When I have a lot of worries,
And my soul is weighted down,
I can almost hear Him saying,
"Only crosses make a crown"
And when my eyes are burning
From the tears that I have shed,
Comes the gentle voice "Remember
What I suffered in thy stead"?

When I look around for comfort,
And there is no listening ear,
Comes a whisper close beside me,
"Hush my child, for I am here"!
And somehow the heavy burden
That I almost couldn't bear,
Slips from off my aching shoulders,
And becomes as light as air.

And my heart is filled with gladness,
And with peace when it recalls,
He knows all things, down to the time
The smallest sparrow falls.
And a new hope stirs within me,
Like the beat of feathered wing,
And in His outstretched arms I find
A love to which I cling.

And I am no longer troubled
At the turning of the ways,
For long ago He told me
"I am with you all the days".
And I find a blessed haven,
Beyond the reach of man,
Just like the tiny sparrow
That He shelters in His hand.

                    Grace E. Easley

A Little Prayer

Every storm that we live through
Is worth another prayer,
After the storm is over
We know that God was there . . .

Every day we've ever lived
Is worth a Thank You to
The God Who keeps our steps with Him—
Who watches all we do . . .

Every small miracle proves that
There's Someone Who must care,
The joys and tears of life always
Are worth a little prayer!

Marion Schoeberlein

Dark Clouds

The dark clouds only last a while
So patient be, and gently smile.
Change can come so swiftly now,
No need for sad and furrowed brow.
Life may be not what you planned,
Frustrations hard to understand,
But Providence reigns up above
So smile, and offer up your love
To One who knows when crosses come,
The best prayer is: "Thy Will be done."

Rev. Thomas Foy

My Friend Forever

When "shades of night" softly gather,
　　as the daylight hours end—
I feel an overwhelming love
　　for God, my dearest Friend.

He walks along beside me
　　in sunshine and in rain.
He laughs with me through happy times,
　　and takes away the pain—
when illness or some sorrow
　　tends to tear my world apart.
The love and comfort He puts forth
　　would melt a hardened heart!

He guides my awkward footsteps
　　along life's rough terrain,
and not one prayer I've said to Him
　　has ever been in vain!

Oh yes, I count my blessings
　　at every long day's end,
for I know God will always be
　　my very dearest Friend!

　　　　　　　Doris A. Orth

Simple Things

Give me the simple things close to my home
   The things that are familiar, old and dear,
I do not have to wander far, or roam
   The Seven Seas — when I have splendor here.

Give me a crackling flame upon the grate
   And the warm smell of bread upon the fire.
I do not have to ride abroad in state
   To find the very core of heart's desire.

A shining tea-pot — friendly hands to pour
   And jam that smells of grapes from our
      own vine.
Could any noble king desire more?
   I am a king myself, for these are mine.

Let those who will seek promised lands afar,
   For treasures so remote I shed no tears.
Why should I strive to reach a distant star
   When heaven with all its beauty is right here!

A Reason to Sing

When I have a heavy burden
And my head is bending low
I carry it straight to Jesus
It's the only place to go.

He can take all the sorrow
With the anxiety, doubts and fears
He can take a heart that's aching
And eyes that are filled with tears.

Replacing it with a rainbow
Neath the shadow of His wings
Suddenly the heart that's aching
Has found a reason to sing!

Dottlee Duggan Reid

A Prayer

O Lord, Thou knowest well how dark the way,
Guide Thou my footsteps, lest they stray;
Give me fresh faith for every hour,
Lest I should ever doubt Thy power
   And make complaint!

Give me the heart, O Lord, strong to endure,
Help me to keep it simple, pure,
Make me unselfish, helpful, true
In every act, whate'er I do,
   And keep content!

Help me to do my share,
Make me courageous, strong to bear
Sunshine or shadow in my life!
Sustain me in the daily strife
   To keep content!

Thank God for life!
  E'en though it bring
    much bitterness and strife,
  And all our fairest hopes
    be wrecked and lost,
  E'en though there be
    more ill than good in life,
  We cling to life
    and reckon not the cost.
Thank God for life!

Put Your Trust in Jesus

Put your trust in Jesus,
Put your trust in Him;
He's the Way, the Truth, the Life,
He'll guide your pathway dim.
For He's a lamp unto our feet,
A light unto our path;
He is the Word that promises
Life to all who ask.

Put your faith in Jesus,
To Him fore'er hold fast;
This world's things shall pass away
But His Word e'er shall last.
So put your trust in Jesus,
New life He'll give to you;
Believe in Him, the Living God . . .
Is all He asks we do.

John 1:12

Loise Pinkerton Fritz

Since life is short,
We need to make it broad.
Since life is brief,
We need to make it bright.

Ella Wheeler Wilcox

A Talk with God

Today I had a talk with God,
Out in a field of goldenrod,
As grasses rippled in the wind,
Some things just needed saying then.
As black birds glistened 'neath the sun,
My little sorrows one by one,
Stirred sleepy wings and flew from me,
Into God's great infinity.

I walked beside a shallow creek,
And through the silence heard Him speak,
And once important things to me,
Seemed smaller than they used to be.
I sat beneath a shady oak,
Where dreams of long ago awoke,
And here within this quiet place,
I met my Maker face to face.

Through forest trail and underbrush,
I heard the plaintive hermit thrush,
Departing from the beaten track,
I got my lost perspective back.
Returning then from whence I came,
I knew my life was not the same,
Since I had talked awhile with God,
Out in the field of goldenrod.

Grace E. Easley

Today

We know nothing of tomorrow
Of its pleasures, joys, or pain,
Yesterday is gone forever
Never to be lived again.
We live today, only today
And should live it carefully
That all we do, and all we say
Should kind and loving be.
Have a smile for each sad mortal
Today you chance to meet
And always have a cheerful word,
For each distressed soul to greet.
Don't let today forever end
Without some good you've done
Today ask our Heavenly Father
To bless us, everyone.

Mary Eleanor Pitney

God's laws are established.
They work with precision:
    A winter turns to spring
    A child becomes an adult
    A bud becomes a flower
    A leaf falls and dies.
No minute is lost in Divine timing;
God's purposes will not be thwarted!

Roxie Lusk Smith

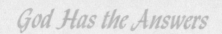

God Has the Answers

Although you're tired and weary
   Just rest the whole night through
As God gives us the mornings
   To see all things anew.

For things look so much brighter
   When they're slept on a while
You wake up in the morning
   And soon you want to smile.

You look and see the sunshine
   The bright blue sky above
You wonder why you fretted
   And you know God is love.

With all this to surround you
    There's naught but this to say
And so with song you praise Him
    Give thanks for this new day.

Yes, God has all the answers
    To problems big and small
We only have to tell Him
    He's at our beck and call.

So we must take our burdens
    And lay them at His feet
Then trust unto His wisdom
    That all our needs He'll meet.

Mary E. Harrington

The Value of Time

Time is such a precious thing
We must value each minute . . .
Bless the world with kindly deeds
The short time we live in it!

Loreta Inman

The World Needs You

God could have made you different
But loves you as you are;
It's good character that matters,
It pleases Him by far.
Each one has capabilities,
Each one is quite unique,
Each has potentialities
That pop out if we seek.
God gave each distinctive gifts
And you have quite a few,
Determine to make use of them,
The world has need of you.

Sr. Mary Gemma Brunke

The Language of Love

Flowers on the mantel,
    Flowers on the sill,
Remind us of the loveliness
    Their presence can fulfill.

Flowers in the garden
    As lovely as can be,
Whisper their contentment
    So obvious to see.

Flowers at the bedside
    Of someone taken ill,
Cheerfully raise the spirit
    Thru their extra special skill.

Flowers on the altar
    In reverence to the Lord,
So proudly testify to
    Their splendorous reward.

Flowers sent to loved ones
    Speak a language all their own;
Help make that precious story
    Of the joys that we have known.

Flowers at the graveside
    Say a last farewell,
In our final statement
    To the ones we loved so well.

Flowers speak the language
    That we fondly know as "love,"
Which isn't any wonder
    For they're sent from God above.

Catherine Janssen Irwin

In the Light of His Love

Let me walk in the light
    of His love;
Let me bask in the glow
    from above.
        Through sunshine and rain,
        in gladness and pain,
Let me walk in the light
    of His love.

Let me live in the light
    of His Word;
Let me lean on the truth
    I have heard.
        When dark shadows roll,
        Let Light flood my soul.
Let me live in the light
    of His Word.

Roxie Lusk Smith

"But he that doeth truth
cometh to the light."
John 3:21.

The Power
of Little Things

The memory of a kindly word
For long gone by,
The fragrance of a fading flower
Sent lovingly,
The gleaming of a sudden smile
Or sudden tear,
The warm pressure of the hand,
The tone of cheer.
The note that only bears a verse
From God's own Word: —
Such tiny things we hardly count
As ministry,
The givers deeming they have shown
Scant sympathy;
But when the heart is overwrought,
Oh, who can tell
The power of such tiny things
To make it well!

Francis Ridley Havergal

The Sentinel

The morning is the gate of day,
  But ere you enter there
See that you set to guard it well,
  The sentinel of prayer.

So shall God's grace your steps attend,
  But nothing else pass through
Save what can give the countersign;
  The Father's will for you.

When you have reached the end of day
  Where night and sleep await,
Set there the sentinel again
  To bar the evening's gate.

So shall no fear disturb your rest,
  No danger and no care.
For only peace and pardon pass
  The watchful guard of prayer.

Where There Is Love

Where there is love the heart is light,
Where there is love the day is bright,
Where there is love there is a song
To help when things are going wrong,
Where there is love there is a smile
To make all things seem more worthwhile,
Where there is love there's quiet peace,
A tranquil place where turmoils cease . . .
Love changes darkness into light
And makes the heart take "wingless flight" —
Oh, blest are they who walk in love . . .
They also walk with God above,
And when man walks with God again
There shall be Peace On Earth for men.

Helen Steiner Rice

Used with permission of
The Helen Steiner Rice Foundation
Suite 2100 Atrium Two
221 E. Fourth St.
Cincinnati, OH 45202

Trust Him

There is One, Who, if we trust Him,
    Guides our like O'er swelling tide:
He came down on earth to save us,
    On the cross for us He died.

Trust Him now! Accept thy Saviour,
    For but He can sin atone:
Trust Him, and when twilight cometh,
    He will not leave thee alone.

Trust him while thy life remaineth,
    He will gladden all thy days.
Trust Him! And for mercies given,
    Ceaseless sing His glorious praise.

                Elwyn C. West

Give Something

Give something that belongs to you,
A friendly word, a smile —
It's like a sunbeam in the blue
Out on a golden isle.

Give something to a suffering soul
That errs the same as you
And cannot find in life its goal,
Your gift will help you, too.

Give something from your heart away
To save a fellow man,
A feeling of warm sympathy
Will do it now and then.

The happiness you will bestow
Today — perhaps tomorrow —
In torrents back again will flow
To help you in your sorrow.

John Tworoger

Seasons of the Heart

The heart has many seasons,
Just as this good old earth,
And they all combine together,
To comprise what we are worth.
There is a childhood innocence,
In which we dream and play,
There is a time for growing up,
And making our own way.

There is a time for keeping,
And a time for letting go,
A time for moving swiftly,
And a time for walking slow.

There is a time for learning,
And a time for teaching, too,
And there is time for resting,
When all the chores are through.

We all know joy and sorrow,
'Tis written in the plan,
But Heaven waits beyond life's gates,
For every earnest man.
Each life has many pictures,
And all a work of art,
But what a silver symphony,
. . . The seasons of the heart.

Grace E. Easley

I sought my soul,
  But my soul I could not see.
I sought my God,
  But my God eluded me.
I sought my brother,
  And I found all three.

Believe within Your Own True Self

Go forth with courage in your heart,
　Dispel all doubt and fear,
And when you need a helping hand
　You'll find God always near.

When failure stares you in the face
　Fight back with might and main,
And if your faith is strong enough
　Your goals you will attain.

Believe within your own true self
　When things look dark for you,
And in the end you're bound to find
　The sun come shining through.

Harold F. Mohn

Have No Fear

If I could strew your pathway
With God's blessings each new day,
I would fence you from all evil
As you pass along life's way.

But there are limits to my power,
I can only do my best.
So, to a Friend who loves you,
Gladly I confide the rest.

Rev. Thomas Foy

Yesterdays

Don't look back to yesterday
For yesterdays are gone
Look to today with a peaceful heart
As each moment you carry on.
Take God's hand as He leads you
On this day you start anew
Walk with Him and talk with Him
He wants to be with you.

Don't look back to yesterday
For yesterdays have past
Look to today with a peaceful mind
With a spiritual thought to last.
Follow God as He takes you
Through each moment one by one
Pray to Him and say to Him
"Lord," let "Thy Will be done."

Carolyn T. Mokan

I Asked for Power

I asked for power
    that I might have the praise of men
I was given weakness,
    that I might feel the need of God . . .

I asked for all things,
    that I might enjoy life
I was given life,
    that I might enjoy all things . . .

I got nothing that I asked for —
    but everything I had hoped for
Almost despite myself, my unspoken
    prayers were answered,

I am among all,
    most richly blessed!

Trust in God

Courage, brother! do not stumble,
   Though thy path be dark as night;
There's a star to guide the humble,
   Trust in God and do the Right.

Norman Macleod

Directions

Jesus, take me by the hand.
Guide me through this troubled land.
When, by storms, I'm tossed about
Calm the waves; erase the doubt.

Dearest Savior, light my way
'Lest in darkness, I might stray.
Though a detour cause concern
May it be a chance to learn.

Oh, Lord, shield me with Your grace.
Hold me in Your sweet embrace.
As a beacon, shining far
Stay my constant, guiding star.

God, without You, I'm afraid
I'd face too many barricades
Wrought with doubts and dead-end streets
Ending in despair, defeats.

Though the path become too steep . . .
And my step a little slow . . .
I know You'll take me in Your keep
When I have nowhere else to go.

Polly Thornton

Life's Wonders

I've never touched a rainbow
And yet I see it there,
Within the sky so far away
Its colors soft and fair,
The wind is quite elusive
And yet I feel its breeze,
And watch it touch the treetops
And gently move the leaves.

Our God within the heavens
I cannot see His face,
And still I feel His presence
And know His saving grace,
The wonders of a rosebud
That opens to the sun,
Each miracle of dawning
And stars when day is done.

The glowing far-off sunset
Untouched by human hands,
So much a part of living
A heart still understands,
We needn't see our Savior
To feel His loving care,
Life's wonders still shall bless us
Each time we kneel in prayer.

Garnett Ann Schultz

Life's Lessons

I learn, as the years roll onward
    And leave the past behind,
That much I had counted sorrow
    But proves that God is kind;
That many a flower I had longed for
    Had hidden a thorn of pain,
And many a rugged bypath
    Led to fields of ripened grain.

The clouds that cover the sunshine
    They can not banish the sun;
And the earth shines out the brighter
    When the weary rain is done.
We must stand in the deepest shadow
    To see the clearest light;
And often thro' wrong's own darkness
    Comes the very strength of light.

The sweetest rest is at even,
   After a wearisome day,
When the heavy burden of labor
   Has born from our hearts away;
And those who have never known sorrow
   Can not know the infinite peace
That falls on the troubled spirit
   When it sees at last release.

We must live thro' the dreary winter
   If we would value the spring;
And the woods must be cold and silent
   Before the robins sing.
The flowers must be buried in darkness
   Before they can bud and bloom,
And the sweetest, warmest sunshine
   Comes after the storm and gloom.

   John Henry Newman

Gratitude

Thank you God, for many things
The hush of dusk, the lark that sings
The warming light as the sun comes up
The golden throat of a buttercup
The scent of pine and new mown hay
The taste of salt in the ocean spray
The sound of hope in a babe's first cry
And for Your hand when I pass by.

Gwen Taft

Sweet Mystery

As days keep unfolding
And seconds tick along
Oh, how priceless the journey
Like a soul with a song.
Oh, how marvelous to gather
These jewels in disguise
Like gems from the heavens
In a package surprise.
The sun in full splendor
Like liquefied gold
Is all ours for the asking
As each new day unfolds.
The glitter of silver
As stars twinkle bright
Is a gift He's releasing
From His heart's beacon light.
So let's rejoice in thanksgiving
And each claim our claim
For God's loving sweet mystery
Will forever remain.

Chris Zambernard

The Precious Book

Though the cover is worn,
And the pages are torn,
And though places bear traces of tears,
Yet more precious than gold
Is the Book worn and old,
That can shatter and scatter my fears.

When I prayerfully look
In the precious old Book,
As my eyes scan the pages I see
Many tokens of love
From the Father above,
Who is nearest and dearest to me.

This old Book is my guide,
'Tis a friend by my side,
It will lighten and brighten my way;
And each promise I find
Soothes and gladdens my mind
As I read it and heed it today.

Fear Not

Have you been thru troubled waters?
   Yes, you have—I know,
Wondering where your God is
   When your spirits seem so low.

The sky looks dark and dreary
   Tho the sun is shining bright.
You're stumbling on a road that's smooth
   But you fail to see the light.

Oh, friend, this too will pass away,
   He'll never let you drown.
For with the strength He gives you
   You'll step on higher ground.

        Helen Parker

Litany of Lovely Things

So runs my litany of lovely things,
That I recite when I have need of words
To cheer my heart and stir my memory,
A cherry orchard bright with humming birds,
The tinkle of a narrow woodland stream,
Over smooth white stones on yellow sand,
Lazy hours on a windy hill,
Where shady oaks and spreading chestnuts stand.

So runs my litany of lovely things,
The long low whistle of a midnight train,
The glow of fireflies through the purple dusk,
The fresh earth smell that follows summer rain.

The scent of jasmine on a restless breeze,
An orange moon about whose shoulders fall
Airy clouds of grey, swept gracefully
Into deep folds that form a star fringed shawl.

Quiet hours when the drowsy hum
Of crickets reach across the edge of sleep,
The soft swish of the waves against the shore,
The ever changing colors of the deep,
The beautiful awareness of a world
To which the Infinite so closely clings,
The mystic vividly made manifest,
. . . So runs my litany of lovely things.

Grace E. Easley

M ay the Lord aid you in the day of trouble.
May He send you help from the holy place.
May we shout with joy over your victory and
May the Lord fulfill all your requests.

More Than a Copy

Jesus within me
wants me to be
more than a copy
of someone I see;
but a loving example,
pure within,
and outwardly reflecting
the image of Him!

Alice Hansche Mortenson

Something Inside

There's something inside
    That makes you go on.
Though the road is rough
    And things go wrong.
There's something that lifts
    Your heart in song.

The world's in a hurry
    Oft' passing you by.
With a lump in your throat
    You wish you could cry,
But something inside
    Keeps your head held high.

No matter how weary
    At the close of the day
There's something inside
    That makes you pray
Asking for courage
    Along life's way.

It dwells in your heart,
    This something inside
Helping you face life
    When you'd rather hide,
It's God's love within you
    Always ready to guide.

Gladys Adkins

I will guide thee.
(Ps. 32:8)

My Prayer

I would lift up my soul to Thee,
That Thou wouldst show the way;
Teach me Thy paths and let me walk
More dutifully each day.
Lead me in truth, Lord, help me know
Thy strength, and help I seek;
Pour forth Thy tender mercies,
For I am tired and weak.
My pride is wounded and I hurt,
My heart is sore with pain.
Deliver me, protect me, Lord,
I ask it in Thy name.

Anna Lee Edwards McAlpin

A Kind Deed Every Day

In the morning with the rising sun,
Think of something to be done,
That will add to others' joy
Free from self and all alloy.

If a burden you make lighter,
And one's life becomes the brighter,
Remember that seed of kindness sown
Will heap up merit all your own.

Be sure you count ere set of sun
One good deed your web has spun;
With your angel then lay it down
To weave for you an immortal crown.

Safe Keeping

Do not look forward to the changes
and chances of this life in fear; rather
look to them with full hope that, as they
arise, God, whose you are, will deliver you
out of them. He is your keeper. He has kept
you hitherto.

Do you but hold fast to His dear hand,
and He will lead you safely through all things;
and, when you cannot stand, He will bear you
in His arms. Do not look forward to what may
happen tomorrow.

Our Father will either shield you from suffering,
or He will give you strength to bear it.

Francis de Sales

After the Storm

Whenever the storm clouds overhead
Loom threatening all around
And darkness hides the sun away
And light cannot be found

Remember that after the darkness,
We treasure more the light
And after the storm is over
The sun comes out more bright.

For that which we lose for a little while
We someday shall regain,
And the gift will be far greater
Than the price we paid in pain.

For God in His great wisdom
May have plans we cannot see
Which for a time are hidden
Away from you and me.

So wait till the storm is over
No matter how dreary and gray
For behind the clouds He's waiting,
To send wonderful things your way.

Jean V. Russell

If the birds can sing
    when all is not fair,
Why is it that we
    are bent down with care?
For God, Who looks down
    on the birds from above,
Is the very same God
    Who keeps us in love.

Charles G. Ramsey

Faith

I do not know what tomorrow may bring.
Maybe I'll cry. Maybe I'll sing.
Maybe I'll be left all alone,
Like an old woman, like an old stone.
Maybe the storm will claim my land,
Maybe I'll feel God's judging Hand,
But if I trust that He's with me
Giving me angels I cannot see
I will have faith to conquer all,
I will not falter, I will not fall,
I do not know what tomorrow may bring,
Maybe I'll cry . . . maybe I'll sing . . .
But if God's on my side I do not care,
I'll win the battle everywhere!

Marion Schoeberlein

I will start anew this morning
　　with a higher, fairer creed;
I will cease to stand complaining
　　of my ruthless neighbor's greed;
I will cease to sit repining while
　　my duty's call is clear;
I will waste no moment whining and
　　my heart shall know no fear.
I will look sometimes about me
　　for the things that merit praise;
I will search for hidden beauties
　　that elude the grumbler's gaze.
I will try to find contentment
　　in the paths that I must tread;
I will cease to have resentment
　　when another moves ahead.
I will not be swayed by envy
　　when my rival's strength is shown;
I will not deny his merit,
　　but I'll try to prove my own;
I will try to see the beauty
　　spread before me, rain or shine;
I will cease to preach your duty
　　and be more concerned with mine.

S. E. Kiser

Judge Ye Not

Judge not thy brother's failings,
Nor ever be the one
To hurl a stone at anything
That he has ever done.
Scorn not his humble efforts,
Nor cast him to the ground,
He may have just discovered
What thou has never found.

Harden not thy heart to tears
That often flow unbidden,
From lonely hearts within whose depths
So much of love is hidden.
Set not thyself as model,
Above thy fellowman,
For charity can open doors,
That pride's key never can.

Be not so self-righteous,
Thy foot can also fall . . .
No man who lives, is blameless,
For sin has touched us all.
And God alone must judge us,
No man has been assigned.
Because the Lord alone can see
Within your heart . . . and mine.

Grace E. Easley

Constant Care

I feel God in the sunshine
And I feel Him in the rain
I know that He remains with me
In good health or in pain.

No matter what the weather
Or the mood within my soul
I know that God is always there
His love to make me whole.

Dolores Karides

Save Utterances for God

Some people talk of their losses;
Some talk of their troubles and pain;
All speak of defeat and of crosses,
But seldom of prosper and gain.

Some total the side of the ledger
That inked in the red of the trial;
They note where their tears spot the pages,
But never keep record of smile.

They grumble of wealth that eludes them,
And whine at their everyday lot,
Instead of recounting the blessings
God's justice and wisdom have brought.

I will not join ranks of complainers
Who barter with pity and trends;
For I've seen enough of God's goodness
To know where His mercy extends.

Roxie Lusk Smith

God Cares!

When His eye is on the sparrow
   And each budding leaf that grows;
When He sends the dew each morning
   And the sunshine to the rose;
You may know beyond all doubting,
   In this trial you're passing through.
God cares . . . and every moment
   He is watching over you!

Keith Bennett

Our Master

Immortal Love, forever full,
　　Forever flowing free,
Forever shared, forever whole,
　　A never-ebbing sea!

Our outward lips confess the name
　　All other names above;
Love only knoweth whence it came,
　　And comprehendeth love.

We may not climb the heavenly steeps
　　To bring the Lord Christ down:
In vain we search the lowest deeps,
　　For Him no depths can drown.

But warm, sweet, tender, even yet
　　A present help is He;
And faith has still its Olivet,
　　And love its Galilee.

The healing of His seamless dress
　　Is by our beds of pain;
We touch Him in life's throng and press,
　　And we are whole again.

Through Him the first fond prayers are said
　　Our lips of childhood frame,
The last low whispers of our dead
　　Are burdened with His name.

O Lord and Master of us all!
　　Whate'er our name or sign,
We own Thy sway, we hear Thy call,
　　We test our lives by Thine.

John Greenleaf Whittier

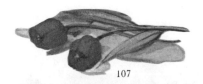

Life Is a Mixture of Sunshine and Rain

Life is a mixture
  of sunshine and rain,
Laughter and teardrops,
  pleasure and pain —
Low tides and high tides,
  mountains and plains,
Triumphs, defeats
  and losses and gains —
But always in all ways
  God's guiding and leading
And He alone knows
  the things we're most needing —

And when He sends sorrow
    or some dreaded affliction,
Be assured that it comes
    with God's kind benediction—
And if we accept it
    as a gift of His love,
We'll be showered with blessings
    from our Father above.

Helen Steiner Rice

Used with permission of:
The Helen Steiner Rice Foundation
Suite 2100 Atrium Two
221 E. Fourth St.
Cincinnati, OH 45202

He Made Me Whole

In the darkest corner of my soul
   a light is shining now,
where a gentle, caring Jesus
   has found His way somehow.

Why He ever wanted to —
   is more than I can see.
So many times I've let Him down.
   Not once has He failed me!

I'm filled with love and gratitude,
   for I know His guiding light
will see me through each trying day,
   and every lonely night.

Where there was once an emptiness —
   my life now — is whole,
since a kind, forgiving Jesus
   found His way into my soul!

Doris A. Orth

The Chapel in the Valley

When it's solitude I'm seeking
　　And from cares I must depart,
To the chapel in the valley
　　I bring my heavy heart.

It is there His peace comes flowing
　　Like the early morning's light,
Bringing soothing comfort
　　And composure back in sight.

I find strength to meet tomorrow
　　From the lessons learned today,
And know my Lord's beside me,
　　Lovingly pointing out the way.

Catherine Janssen Irwin

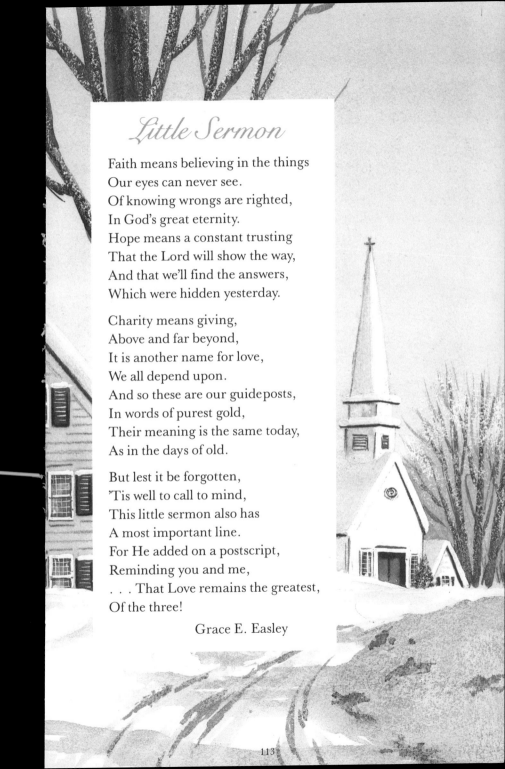

Little Sermon

Faith means believing in the things
Our eyes can never see.
Of knowing wrongs are righted,
In God's great eternity.
Hope means a constant trusting
That the Lord will show the way,
And that we'll find the answers,
Which were hidden yesterday.

Charity means giving,
Above and far beyond,
It is another name for love,
We all depend upon.
And so these are our guideposts,
In words of purest gold,
Their meaning is the same today,
As in the days of old.

But lest it be forgotten,
'Tis well to call to mind,
This little sermon also has
A most important line.
For He added on a postscript,
Reminding you and me,
 . . . That Love remains the greatest,
Of the three!

Grace E. Easley

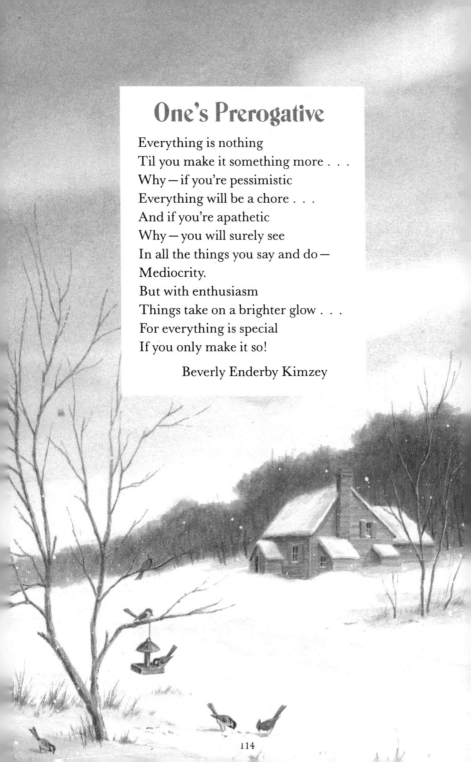

One's Prerogative

Everything is nothing
Til you make it something more . . .
Why — if you're pessimistic
Everything will be a chore . . .
And if you're apathetic
Why — you will surely see
In all the things you say and do —
Mediocrity.
But with enthusiasm
Things take on a brighter glow . . .
For everything is special
If you only make it so!

Beverly Enderby Kimzey

Eternal Flame

Today I lit a candle
On the altar of my heart,
And I prayed the glow within me
Would ignite a magic spark.

A flame to burn forever
So that always I will see,
A world that's filled with beauty
Because He glows in me.

Chris Zambernard

Keep Me Near Thee, Dearest Jesus

Keep me near Thee, dearest Jesus,
　　Always in Thy holy sight.
Draw me ever closer to Thee
　　'Till the coming of the night.

Hold my hand and lead me onward
　　Through the trials and stress of day:
Let me see Thee, hear Thee, feel Thee —
　　In my daily toil and play.

Hand in Thine I can not falter
　　Thou art ever at my side;
And my heavy heart seems lighter
　　When it in Thy heart confides.

Let me live in Thy dear presence
　　Trusting Thee in woe or weal;
And remember when life hurts most
　　'Tis Thy wounded hand I feel.

Today I Give Thanks

So many blessings come my way,
From morning 'til the close of day,
Wherever I am, whatever the time,
Appreciation floods my mind!

I count the good things I have in store,
There's so much to be thankful for!
My heart's overwhelmed and I must raise
My voice in gratitude and praise!

"Thank You, God, for joy in my soul,
For guiding, for healing, for making me whole! . . .
For unexpected pleasures, dropped from above,
For unlimited measures of caring and love!"

"Thank You for Your vibrant presence, too,
In the thoughtful comments of others who
Make me feel special and worthwhile . . .
For a friendly hug, and a loving smile!"

I will not wait for a certain time,
I'll dedicate each day that's mine,
To expressing thanks to God . . . This way
Each day will be "Thanksgiving Day"!

Micky Meyer Mathewson

God bless our home, and help us
 To love each other true;
To make our home the kind of place
 Where everything we do
Is filled with love and kindness,
 A dwelling place for Thee,
And help us, God, each moment,
 To live most helpfully.

I Am the Clay

The more I try to give away,
    The more God fills me every day.
As I empty my loving cup,
    He's always there to fill it up.

He who turned water into wine
    Has filled my life with love divine.
All that I am, or hope to be,
    Reflects the love He's given me.

He is the Potter; I'm the clay,
    Shaped and molded day by day
To be a vessel of His love
    Filled here on earth by God above.

Clay Harrison

A Benediction

God keep thee in the busy day,
    And in night's lonely hour;
Though storms may gather 'round thy way,
    Trust His protecting power.

God guide thee! May His wisdom shine
    Unclouded o'er thy soul,
And lead thee by its light divine
    To the eternal goal.

'Tis morning! and I find myself
Within another day,
This day, a gift of God to me,
The hope of yesterday!

And, Holy Father, now I come,
So early in the morning,
To give You honor, love and praise,
Your holiness adorning.

And as I lift my heart to You
In prayer and praise and love,
In turn I feel Your loving grace
Flowing from above,

Establishing this bright new day
With joy and love and power;
And so I consecrate each day
This sacred quiet hour!

Helen Neimy

Let the Morning Come Through

With your face to the sun,
Let the morning come through:
The bright golden sunbeams,
The crystals of dew . . .

The sky full of heavens,
The forests alive
With beauties unnumbered
That gladden the eye . . .

The crow of the rooster,
The cackling of hens,
The babbling of brooklets
That flow through the glens.

With your face to the sun,
Let the morning come through,
For God in His glory
Is speaking to you.

Loise Pinkerton Fritz

Reach Out

Why go in search of beauty
To all those foreign lands,
When there's a wealth of loveliness
So very close at hand.

Just step outside your doorway
And see the birds in flight
Or watch the sun in early morn
Turn darkness into light.

Not far beyond your reaching hands
Are trees so straight and tall,
Rustled by a gentle breeze
They sing their song to all.

Who gives these treasures to us?
It is our Savior's plan.
You'll never need to search for Him
He's right there where you stand.

Albert N. Theel

God Speed You
on Life's Way

Christ walk with thee,
    beloved Friend,
His Blessing rare
    thy life attend,
What sweeter greeting
    could I send?

All wishes are enclosed in this;
    Possessing Him, no grace thou'lt miss,
Whose Presence is the soul's true bliss.

Christ walk with thee in love to share
    Thy every joy and grief and care,
To bless thy life with gifts most rare.

Loving Service

Dream not the sunny hours away,
  Be up and doing ever,
For life is short and after life,
  There comes the vast Forever.
And single not great work to do,
  A word that's kindly spoken,
A smile, a glance may help to heal
  The heart that's nearly broken.

If happiness should dwell with you
  Or sorrow be your guest,
It matters not, put self aside
  And bravely do your best.
The sunshine shed on other lives
  Will surely gild your own,
And harvest time will bring to you
  The seed which you have sown.

Then haste to do the Master's work.
  The cup of water giving,
And soon with thankful heart you'll find
  That life is worth the living.
Dream not the sunny hours away,
  Be up and doing ever
For life is short and after life
  There comes the vast Forever.

The Power of Prayer

Joy in the midst of trial
Can be ours, if we stop to pray.
God listens to every plea
And gives us strength for the day.
'Though we may not always receive
The things we are asking for,
In prayer there is hope and relief,
When troubles knock at the door.
Prayer, like a soothing balm,
Quiets the heart and soul,
Restoring peace and calm
And joy, to make us whole.

Elsie Natalie Brady

Time Is Precious

If there's a deed you've left undone
  Before the setting of the sun —
    Do it now!

If there are words you didn't speak
  To soothe a hurt or boost the weak —
    Do it now!

If you can make a sick friend well,
  Or just a happy story tell —
    Do it now!

Time is precious every day —
  Make it count in a selfless way.

    Catherine Janssen Irwin

Friendship

Friendship is a mighty ship
That weathers many gales,
And leaves a blessing to the world
In every place it sails.

It helps the dreary, cheers the sad,
And drives dark clouds away.
It gives a helping hand to those
Who've fallen by the way.

Friendship is a blessed ship
That's full of peace and love,
And carries sunshine everywhere,
From God's own home above.

It makes the world a better place,
Even more like heaven sweet —
And helps to smooth the pathways out,
For weary pilgrims' feet.

Karen Mutsch